festive
IRIS
folding

**Maruscha Gaasenbeek
and Tine Beauveser**

FORTE PUBLISHERS

Contents

ISBN 90 5877 177 6
NUR 475

This is a publication from
Forte Publishers BV
Boothstraat 1c
3512 BT Utrecht
The Netherlands

For more information about the
creative books available from
Forte Publishers:
www.hobby-party.com

Editor: Marianne Perlot
Final editing: Hanny Vlaar
Photography and digital image
editing: Fotografie Gerhard Witteveen,
Apeldoorn, the Netherlands
Cover and inner design:
Studio Herman Bade BV, Baarn,
the Netherlands

Preface	3
Techniques	4
Step-by-step	5
Materials	7
Circles	8
Playing with circles	11
Tulips	14
Chickens	18
Apples	20
Party!	23
Socks	26
Hearts	30

Preface

Iris folding has slowly but surely spread through the Netherlands. It started in a small group with a couple of workshops and was spread by the participants. It was enthusiastically taken up by everybody who was pleased with this new, enjoyable folding activity. Iris folding does not have to cost any money, since you can simply use old envelopes. Open your post and look at the inside of the envelope: blue, red, green, plain or with all kinds of figures: such as stars, dots, horses, checks, knitting patterns, stripes, tiger prints, blocks, birds, dolls. Insurance companies, banks, government bodies, companies, universities and museums often print their own logo in their envelopes. We have already collected over THREE HUNDRED different envelopes!

Ask your family and friends to collect envelopes for you. Their initial surprise will quickly turn to enthusiasm when they see the attractive cards you make with the pieces of paper you cut into strips. IRIS folders will be happy with a bag of used envelopes. And they will surprise the people who save their envelopes for them with a pretty IRIS folded card! Spending an afternoon working with other IRIS folders will give you new possibilities: you can take your doubles with you and swap them. This will leave you with even more different envelopes and, thus, increase your options. We had a lot of fun coming up with and drawing the new patterns in this book. But what we enjoyed most was spending a couple of hours selecting envelope paper, cutting it into strips and then sticking these strips onto a card. That's IRIS folding!

Have fun!

Maruscha   *Tine*

Thanks:
Jaap and Geert for their stimulation and thoughts, and for listening to everything about IRIS folding.
Lianne, Catrien, Hans, Leida, Tjeerd and Pietie for their involvement and for collecting envelopes.

Techniques

The starting point for IRIS folding is the pattern. Cut the outer shape of the pattern out of the card and then fill the hole from the outside to the inside with folded strips of used envelopes. You will be working on the reverse side of your card, so in fact you will be working on a mirror image; when you have finished, you stick it onto another card. For a round pattern, select four different envelopes where the patterns and colours combine and contrast nicely. Cut all the envelopes into strips in the same way, for example, from left to right. The number of strips you will need depends on the pattern; you will need between four and eight strips. The width of the strips also depends on the pattern and is stated for each card.

First, you need to fold the edge of the strips over and sort them into each different type of envelope. Next, you cover each section in turn by following the numbers (1, 2, 3, 4, 5, etc), so that you rotate the design.

Lay the strips with the fold facing towards the middle of the pattern and then stick them on the left-hand and right-hand sides of the card using adhesive tape. Finally, stick on an attractive piece of deco tape to cover the hole in the middle. Avoid colour differences by using one envelope for the same design.

The circle (see card 1 in chapter 1)

The most important thing is to start with the basic circle, because from this, you will learn the unique folding and sticking technique needed for all the patterns. The cards in this book get increasingly difficult. Therefore, start at the beginning. You will notice that you'll quickly get used to the technique of IRIS folding.

Preparation

1. Lay the card (13.2 x 9.3 cm) down with the back facing towards you.
2. Draw two pencil lines through the middle of the card. These lines will help you determine the place for your pattern.
3. Adjust the circle cutter to Ø 6 cm.
4. Place the circle cutter on the cross point of the two pencil lines on your card and cut the circle out.
5. Copy the basic circle pattern 1 from this book and tape it to your cutting mat.
6. Place the card on top with the hole exactly over the pattern (you should be looking at the back of the card) and stick the left-hand side to your cutting mat using a couple of pieces of masking tape.
7. Choose four envelopes with different patterns. Four different blue envelopes have

1. The inside of more than THREE HUNDRED envelopes.

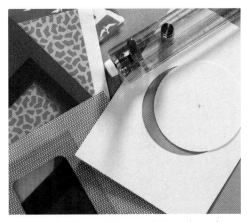

2. Cut the circle out of the back of the card. Cut the envelopes into strips and fold the edge over.

3. Place the pattern on your cutting mat. Place the card on top and secure the left-hand side into place. Place the strips precisely against the line and stick the left-hand and right-hand sides in place using adhesive tape.

4. Fold the card open from time to time to see whether the patterns you have made continue nicely.

been used for the card shown in the top left-hand corner.

8. Cut 2 cm wide strips from these envelopes (either lengthways or widthways) and make separate piles of colour A, colour B, colour C and colour D.

9. For each strip, fold a border (approximately 7 mm) along the entire length with the nice side facing outwards.

IRIS folding

10. Take a folded strip of colour A and place this over section 1, exactly against the line of the pattern with the folded side facing towards the middle. Allow 0.5 cm to stick out on the left-hand and right-hand sides and cut the rest off. By doing so, the strip will also slightly stick out over the edge of the pattern at the bottom, so that section 1 is totally covered.

11. Stick it to the card on the left-hand and right-hand sides using a small piece of adhesive tape, but remain 0.5 cm from the side of the card.

12. Take a strip of colour B and place it on section 2 on the pattern. Tape this to the left-hand and right-hand sides of the card.

13. Take a strip of colour C. Place this on section 3 and stick it into place.

14. Take a strip of colour D. Place this on section 4 and stick it into place.

15. You have now gone all the way around. Start again with colour A on section 5, colour B on section 6, colour C on section 7 and colour D on section 8.

The strips on sections 1, 5, 9, 13, 17 and 21 of this pattern are all of colour A. The strips on sections 2, 6, 10, 14, 18 and 22 are all of colour B. The strips on sections 3, 7, 11, 15, 19 and 23 are all of colour C. The strips on sections 4, 8, 12, 16, 20 and 24 are all of colour D.

Finishing

After section 24, carefully remove the card and look at what you have made. Stick a single piece of deco tape in the middle on the back of the card. You can use punches, figure scissors, embossing stencils, etc. to finish the card. Stick small pieces of double-sided adhesive tape along the borders. Remove the protective layer and fix your design on a double card. Do not use glue, because all the paper strips place pressure on the card.

Cutting decorative borders

To cut the card using figure scissors, a pencil line is drawn on the back of the card 0.5 cm

Materials

To make the cards:
- ❏ Card: Canson Mi-Teintes (C), Artoz (A) and Papicolor (P)
- ❏ Cutting knife, Cutting mat
- ❏ Pencil
- ❏ Ruler with a metal cutting edge (Securit)
- ❏ Adhesive tape
- ❏ Double-sided adhesive tape
- ❏ Masking tape
- ❏ Various punches (TomTas, Craft Punch)
- ❏ Multi-corner punch (Reuser)
- ❏ Hand punch: flower and small hearts (Fiskars)
- ❏ Hole punch
- ❏ Scissors and silhouette scissors
- ❏ Figure scissors and corner scissors (Fiskars)
- ❏ Ornare Baby decorative pricking template (Marianne Design)
- ❏ Circle cutter
- ❏ Gel pen
- ❏ Photo glue
- ❏ Pink pencil
- ❏ Embossing pen
- ❏ Various embossing stencils (Avec, Linda Design, Make Me!)
- ❏ Light box

IRIS folding
- ❏ Strips of used envelopes

The middle
- ❏ Deco tape
- ❏ Holographic paper

from the side. Cut along the line using the teeth of the scissors. Fold the cut part backwards and carefully place the teeth of the scissors in the pattern which has already been cut out. This will create a border which continues in one smooth line.

Embossing
To emboss, place the stencil on the good side of the card and secure it in place using masking tape. Place the card (with the stencil) upside down on the light box. Carefully press the paper through the opening in the stencil using an embossing pen. You only have to push around the edge to raise up the whole image.

The patterns
Full-size examples of all the patterns are given in this book. Copy them using the light box. Their large size makes the patterns easy to cut out from the card. A useful aid for copying the patterns onto the card is the transparent plastic IRIS folding and drawing template. This A4-size template has five different patterns. Specially punched cards are available for the tulip, chicken, apple and heart patterns.

Circles

Circles in different

colours and flavours!

For all cards, follow the instructions for the basic circle (see Techniques)

Card 1

Card: cornflower blue A425 (14.8 x 21 cm) and lilac C104 (13.2 x 9.3 cm) • Pattern 1 • 2 cm wide strips from 4 different blue envelopes • Silver holographic paper • Circle cutter
Cut a Ø 6 cm circle in the middle of the lilac paper.

Card 2

Card: honey yellow A243 (13 x 26 cm and 10 x 10 cm) • Pattern 1 • 2 cm wide strips from 4 different beige and brown envelopes • Gold deco tape • Circle cutter
Cut a Ø 6 cm circle out from the inside of the left-hand half of the card. After finishing the IRIS folding, cover the design with the small card. Cutting tip for decorating: cut 1 mm strips of envelope paper. They will curl up themselves into a nice curve.

Card 3

Card: violet C507 (14.8 x 21 cm) and lilac C104 (12.8 x 9 cm) • Pattern 1 • 2 cm wide strips from 4 different purple envelopes, such as from advertising, an internet provider and a university • Silver holographic paper • Circle cutter

Card 4

Card: lilac C104 (14.8 x 21 cm) and violet C507 (13 x 9 cm) • Pattern 1 • 2 cm wide strips from 4 different purple envelopes from a university, hospital, wine guild and insurance company • Silver holographic paper • Circle cutter

Card 5

Card: aquamarine A363 (13 x 26 cm and 10 x 10 cm) • Pattern 1 • 2 cm wide strips from 4 different aquamarine envelopes • 11 x 11 cm envelope paper (colour A) • Silver deco tape • Circle cutter
After the IRIS folding, decorate the front of the card with circles of envelope paper. Cutting tip: first, cut the circles out to Ø 10 cm and then cut them to Ø 9.6 cm. Cut the small circle to Ø 8 cm and then to Ø 7.6 cm. Place them around the circle you have just made and stick them in place using a small amount of glue.

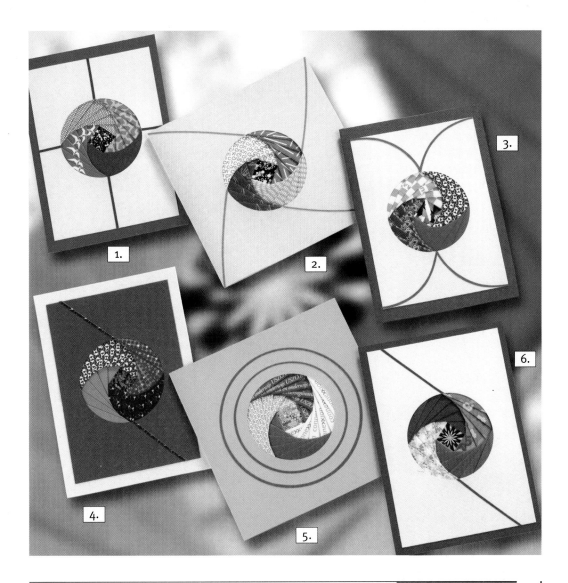

Card 6

*Card: azure C590 (14.8 x 21 cm) and soft blue C102
(14 x 9.5 cm) • Pattern 1 • 2 cm wide strips from 4
different blue and green envelopes • Silver deco
tape • Circle cutter*

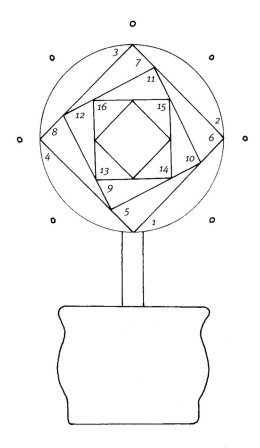

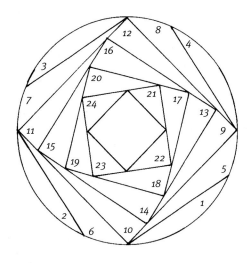

pattern 1

pattern 2

Playing with circles

These round trees

love the sun.

The sun is made according to the description for card 1.

Card page 3: pattern 2 with materials from the tulip card on the front cover (page 15).

Card 1

Card: honey yellow A243 (14.8 x 21 cm) and lobster red A545 (14 x 9.8 cm) • Pattern 2 • 2 cm wide strips from 4 different brown and orange envelopes • 10 x 10 cm envelope paper (colour B). Gold holographic paper • Circle cutter • Cloud corner punch

Cut a Ø 5 cm circle out of the middle of the red card and punch out the corners. Turn pattern 2 45 degrees anticlockwise, so that section 1 is horizontal. Follow the instructions given for the basic circle. Cutting tip: copy half of the sun ray border on the right-hand side of the back of the envelope paper. Fold it in two and stick it together with staples. Cut out the sun rays first and then the semicircle. Stick the sun on the card.

Card 2

Card: honey yellow A243 (14.8 x 21 cm), dark blue A417 (14 x 10 cm) and light yellow A241 (13.7 x 9.5 cm) • Pattern 2 • 2 cm wide strips from 4 different yellow and beige envelopes • 10 x 10 cm envelope paper (colour A) • Gold holographic paper • Circle cutter • Victorian embossing stencil

Emboss the smallest card.

Card 3

Card: blue and orange duo-colour card (14.8 x 21 cm) and a covering circle (Ø 9 cm) of the same material • Pattern 2 • 2 cm wide strips from 4 different yellow envelopes • 10 x 10 cm orange envelope paper • Copper red deco tape • Circle cutter

bow

halo

• *Regal corner scissors* • *Sun mini punch*
Cut the Ø 5 cm circle out of the left-hand inner card. Cut two corners using the corner scissors. Punch out orange suns.

Card 4

Card: butter yellow C400 (14.8 x 21 cm) and royal blue A427 (11.7 x 9.7 cm) • Pattern 2 • 2 cm wide strips from 4 different orange and yellow envelopes • 10 x 10 cm envelope paper (colour C) • Gold deco tape • Circle cutter • Sun embossing stencil • Regal corner scissors
Cut the corners of the blue card and cut out the circle. Emboss the corners of the yellow card.

Card 5

Card: off-white C335 (14.8 x 21 cm) and dark green C448 (14.4 x 10 cm) • Pattern 2 • 2 cm wide strips from 4 different red and green envelopes • Gold holographic paper • Flower hand punch • Bow punch
Cut a Ø 5 cm circle out of the left-hand inner card approximately 5.5 cm from the top. Punch out flowers along the edge of the circle. Cover these with pieces of envelope paper and finish it off as described for a basic circle. Cover the worked area with the small card. Copy the flower pot and the stem onto the back of the envelope paper. Cut them out and stick them on the card together with the bow and the flowers.

1.

2.

5.

6.

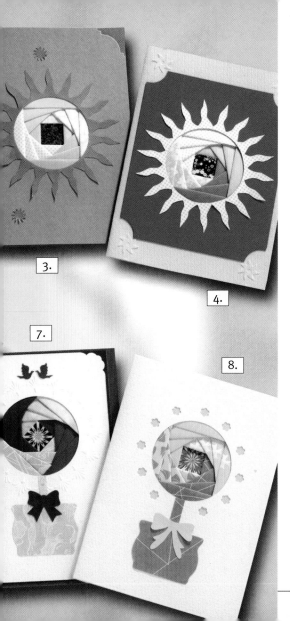

3.

4.

7.

8.

Card 6

Card: resin brown C336 (14.8 x 21 cm) and dark pink C350 (13.7 x 9.5 cm) • Pattern 2 • 2 cm wide strips from 4 different pink and beige envelopes • Gold deco tape • Round flower frame embossing stencil • Pink pencil

Cut the Ø 5 cm circle out of the pink card and emboss the border. Colour in the flowers.

Card 7

Card: cerise P33 (14.8 x 21 cm) and carnation white P03 (14.2 x 8.8 cm) • 14.5 x 9.3 cm purple envelope paper • Pattern 2 • 2 cm wide strips from 4 different purple, lilac, red and beige enve-lopes • Silver deco tape • Victorian embossing stencil • Flower corner punch • Bow punch • Dove hand punch

Cut the Ø 5 cm circle out of the white card. Emboss the border and punch out two corners. Punch out the doves and the bow.

Card 8

Card: lemon yellow C101 (14.8 x 21 cm) and almond green C480 (14.6 x 10.3 cm) • Pattern 2 • 2 cm wide strips from 4 different green envelopes • Silver deco tape • Flower hand punch

Rotate pattern 2 45 degrees anticlockwise so that section 1 is horizontal.

Tulips

Spring is in the air.

All the cards are made according to the description given for card 1.

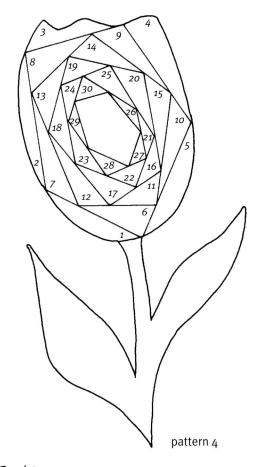

pattern 4

Card on the front cover

Card: bright red C506 (14.8 x 21 cm), light orange C553 (14.4 x 9.3 cm) and white (14 x 8.6 cm) • Pattern 5 • 2 cm wide strips from 5 different orange and red envelopes • 6 x 6 cm green envelope paper • Silver deco tape

Card 1

Card: dark blue (14.8 x 21 cm), lilac C507 (14.2 x 9.7 cm) and ivory C111 (14 x 9.5 cm) • Pattern 4 • 2 cm wide strips from 5 different green, pink-red and purple envelopes • 6 x 6 cm envelope paper (colour A) • Gold holographic paper • Multi-corner punch • Text embossing stencil

Punch out the corners, emboss the text and cut the flower out of the ivory card. Finish it off as described for a basic circle.

Copy the stem and the leaves onto the back of the envelope paper (colour A) using the light box. Cut these out and stick them onto the front.

Card 2

Card: shell-white C112 (14.8 x 21 cm), beige C374 (13.5 x 9.4 cm) and indigo blue C140 (13 x 8.7 cm) • Pattern 4 • 2 cm wide strips from 5 different beige envelopes • 6 x 6 cm envelope paper (colour A) •

pattern 3

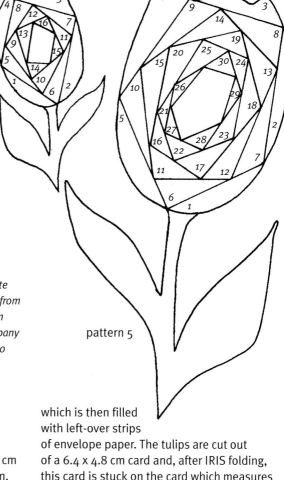

Gold holographic paper • Butterfly corner punch
Punch out the top corners of the blue card.

Card 3

*Card: dark green C448 (14.8 x 21 cm), butter
yellow C400 (13.4 x 9.2 cm) and off-white C335
(13 x 8.8 cm) • Pattern 5 • 2 cm wide strips
from 5 different yellow and green envelopes •
6 x 6 cm envelope paper (colour A) • Gold deco
tape • Tulip punch*
Punch the tulips out of the white card.

Card 4

*Card: dark green C448 (14.8 x 21 cm) and lily-white
C110 (14.2 x 9.5 cm) • Pattern 4 • 2 cm wide strips from
5 different purple, pink and green envelopes from
Foster Parents, a wine guild and an insurance company
• 6 x 6 cm envelope paper (colour A) • Flamed deco
tape • Ornamental corner punch • Tulip punch*
Punch out the corners of the white card.
Punch the small tulips out of the envelope
paper (colour A).

pattern 5

Labels (patterns 3, 10 and 14)

Almost all the labels are made out of a 7 x 11 cm
card and a cover card measuring 6.8 x 5.2 cm.
The shape of both the flag and the heart are
cut out of the inner left-hand side of the card,
which is then filled
with left-over strips
of envelope paper. The tulips are cut out
of a 6.4 x 4.8 cm card and, after IRIS folding,
this card is stuck on the card which measures
7 x 11 cm. The final size of the gift labels is
7 x 5.5 cm.

1.

2.

3.

4.

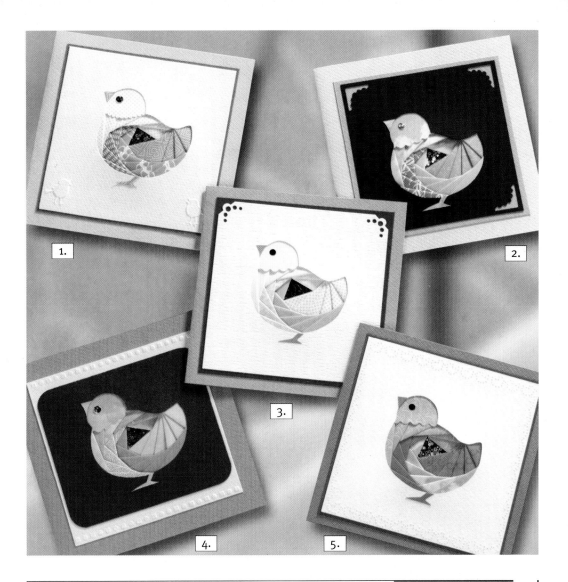

Chickens

Spring: a time for new life!

All the cards are made according to the description given for card 1.

Card 1

Card: butter yellow C400 (13.3 x 26.6 cm), salmon beige C384 (11.4 x 11.4 cm) and lily-white C110 (11.1 x 11.1 cm) • Pattern 6 • 2 cm wide strips from 4 different orange, beige and yellow envelopes • 3 x 3 cm envelope paper (colour D) • Gold deco tape • Hole punch • Mini shell figure scissors • Spring embossing stencil

Emboss two birds and cut the chicken shape out of the back of the white card (not the beak or the feet). For section 4a, use the figure scissors to cut a border along one side of the envelope paper which measures 3 x 3 cm; this piece will not be folded. Fill the chicken with strips according to the instructions for a basic circle. Note that colour A stops at section 17, therefore, section 21 is not included. Cut the beak and the feet out of the envelope paper (colour C). Make the eye from deco tape using the hole punch.

Card 2

Card: dark pink C350 (13.3 x 26.6 cm), golden yellow C374 (11 x 11 cm) and indigo blue C140 (10.3 x 10.3 cm) • Pattern 6 • 2 cm wide strips from 4 different soft orange and yellow envelopes • 3 x 3 cm envelope paper (colour D) • Gold deco tape • Hole

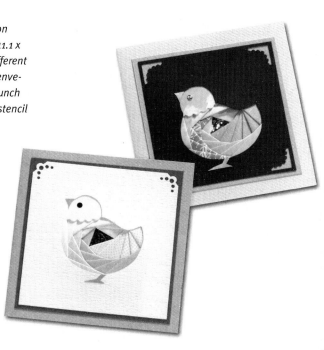

punch • Shell figure scissors • Flower corner punch

Punch out the corners and cut out the chicken from the blue card.

Card 3

Card: sienna C374 (13 x 26 cm), bright red C506 (11.5 x 11.5 cm) and off-white (11 x 11 cm) • Pattern 6 • 2 cm wide strips from 4 different yellow envelopes • 3 x 3 cm envelope paper (colour D) • Gold holographic paper • Hole punch • Shell figure scissors • Multi-corner punch

Punch out the top corners and cut out the chicken from the white card.

Card 4

Card: almond green C480 (13.3 x 26.6 cm), ivory C111 (10.8 x 10.8 cm) and dark green C448 (9 x 10.5 cm) • Pattern 6 • 2 cm wide strips from 4 different beige, yellow and soft green envelopes • 3 x 3 cm envelope paper (colour D) • Gold deco tape • Hole punch • Shell figure scissors • Regal corner punch • Geometric embossing stencil

Cut out the corners and cut out the chicken from the dark green card.

Emboss the top and bottom border of the white card.

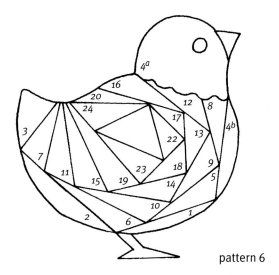

pattern 6

Card 5

Card: light orange C553 (13 x 26 cm), lavender blue C150 (11.8 x 11.8 cm) and off-white (11.4 x 11.4 cm) • Pattern 6 • 2 cm wide strips from 4 different orange envelopes • 3 x 3 cm envelope paper (colour D) • Gold deco tape • Hole punch • Shell figure scissors • Baby decorative pricking stencil

Place the decorative pricking stencil on the back of the white card. Prick the chickens along the top and bottom and prick a decorative border along the sides.

Apples

Nice juicy apples!

All the cards are made according to
the instructions given for card 1.
Four different envelopes are used
in each apple.

Card 1 *(also shown on the cover)*

*Card: apple green C475 (13 x 26 cm), dark
green C448 (10.5 x 10.5 cm) and off-white
C335 (10 x 10 cm) • Pattern 7 • 2 cm wide
strips from 4 different green envelopes •
Gold deco tape*

Cut the apple from the white card (not
the stem or the leaves). Do the IRIS folding
as described for the basic circle.
Copy the stem, the leaves and the calyx
onto the back of green envelope paper.
Cutting tip: turn the paper using the hand
which holds the paper.
Stick the cut out pieces above and below
the apple.

Card 2

*Card: dark green C448 (13.3 x 26.6 cm), resin
brown C336 (10.5 x 10.5 cm) and off-white C335*

1.

3.

2.

(10 x 10 cm) • Pattern 7 • 2 cm wide strips from different beige, light orange, red and grey-green envelopes • Gold holographic paper • Ornamental embossing stencil
Emboss the corners of the smallest card.

Card 3

Card: green (13 x 26 cm) and off-white C335 (11 x 11 cm) • Pattern 7 • 2 cm wide strips from different beige, light orange, red and grey-green envelopes from, for example, a publisher, insurance company and wine guild • Silver deco tape • Multi-corner punch
Punch out the corners of the white card and cut out the apple.

Card 4

Card: dark green C448 (13 x 26 cm), almond green C480 (12 x 12 cm) and off-white C335 (11 x 11 cm) • Pattern 7 • 2 cm wide strips from different green, grey and light yellow envelopes • Silver deco tape • Regal corner scissors
Cut the corners of the almond green card with the corner scissors.
Round off the corners of the white card using the corner scissors and cut out the apple.

4.

pattern 7

pattern 8

Party!

A party hat, flags and a balloon.

The drawing of the balloon (pattern 11) is shown on page 32.

Card 1

Card: white (14.8 x 21 cm), orange (13.9 x 9.7 cm) and red (13.4 x 9.2 cm) • Pattern 9 • 2 cm wide strips from 4 different blue and red envelopes • Silver holographic paper • Multi-corner punch

Punch out the right-hand corners and cut out the flag from the back of the red card. Fill the flag with strips.

Cut the flagpole out of blue envelope paper and stick it on the card.

Card 2

Card: azure P04 (14.8 x 21 cm) and white (13.8 x 9.5 cm) • Pattern 11 • 2 cm wide strips of 4 aquamarine envelopes • Silver holographic paper • Balloon punch • Embroidery silk

Cut the balloon from the white paper.

Card 3

Card: azure C590 (14.8 x 21 cm) and white (13 x 9.5 cm) • Pattern 8 • 2 cm wide strips from 3

different blue envelopes • Silver holographic paper • Multi-corner punch • Mini shell figure scissors

Punch out the corners of the white card and cut out the hat. Decorate the bottom with a border of envelope paper.

Cutting tip: fold 2 x 4 cm of envelope paper double so that it measures 2 x 2 cm and cut the half feather along the line of the fold.

Card 4

Card: carnation white P03 (14.8 x 21 cm) and turquoise C595 (13.5 x 9 cm) • Pattern 11 • 2 cm wide strips from 4 different green and yellow envelopes • Silver holographic paper • Multi-corner punch • Embroidery silk

Punch out the corners of the smallest card.

Card 5

Card: azure P04 (14.8 x 21 cm) and off-white (12.8 x 9.6 cm) • 13.2 x 10 cm envelope paper (colour D) • Pattern 9 • 2 cm wide strips from 4 different blue envelopes • Silver holographic paper • Multi-corner punch

Punch out the right-hand corners.

Card 6

Card: white (14.8 x 21 cm) and blue (14.6 x 10.3 cm) • Pattern 9 • 2 cm wide strips from 4 different red,

white and blue envelopes • Silver
holographic paper • Scrap pieces of
red and blue card
Cut the flag out of the left-hand
inner card. After the IRIS folding,
cover with the blue card. Decorate
with the scrap pieces
of card.

Card 7

*Card: red C505 (14.8 x 21 cm) and white
(13.8 x 9.5 cm) • Pattern 11 • 2 cm wide
strips from 4 different red envelopes •
Silver holographic paper • Butterfly embossing stencil • Butterfly punch • Regal corner
scissors • Embroidery silk*
Cut round corners and cut the balloon
out of the white card. Emboss the
butterflies. Stick the punched out
butterflies on the embossed butterflies.

Card 8

*Card: carnation white P03 (14.8 x 21 cm) and IRIS
blue P31 (13.2 x 9 cm) • Pattern 8 • 2 cm wide strips
of 3 purple and white envelopes • Silver deco tape •
Mini shell figure scissors • Diamond corner punch*
Punch out the corners and cut the hat from the
blue card.

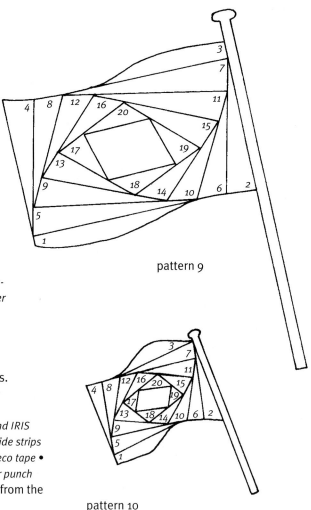

pattern 9

pattern 10

Socks

For the cutest baby.

All the socks are made according to the description given for card 1.

Card 1

Card: Havana brown C502 (13 x 26 cm) and dark pink C350 (11.6 x 11.6 cm) • Pattern 12 • 2 cm wide strips from 4 different yellow and brown envelopes • 3 x 5 cm envelope paper (colour D) • Gold deco tape • Hole punch • Small heart hand punch • Feet and washing line embossing stencils • 30 cm cream ribbon • Copper coloured bell

Emboss the washing line and the feet in the small card. Only cut out the foot part of the sock from the small card. Use a light box to draw the leg (B) on the back of the piece of envelope paper (colour D) and cut it out. Use photo glue to stick it on the front of the card so that it joins the hole of the foot. Wait until the glue is dry and then punch out the hearts as shown in the diagram. After the IRIS folding, thread the ribbon through the hearts and tie it in a bow. Cut the small oval out of envelope paper (colour A) and stick it on the top of part B. Tie the bell onto the ribbon using a piece of

cotton. Punch a hole in the top left-hand corner and make an eye through which to hang the card up using the rest of the ribbon.

Card 2

Card: azure P04 (13 x 26 cm), P32 (11.3 x 11.3 cm) and pastel green A331 (10.7 x 10.7 cm) • Pattern 12 • 2 cm wide strips from 4 different green, aqua and white envelopes • 3 x 5 cm envelope paper (colour C) • oval (colour A) • Silver holographic paper • Hole punch • Small heart hand punch • Ornare baby decorative

pricking template • 30 cm aqua-coloured ribbon
Prick a chicken border along the top and bottom of the smallest card.

Card 3

Card: light pink C103 (13 x 26 cm) • pink C352 (11 x 11 cm) and lily-white C110 (10.3 x 10.3 cm) • Pattern 12 • 2 cm wide strips from 4 different pink, red and purple envelopes • 3 x 5 cm envelope paper (colour C) • Oval (colour A) • Silver deco tape • Hole punch • Small heart hand punch • Baby embossing stencil • 30 cm pink ribbon
Emboss the white card.

Card 4

Card: indigo blue C140 (13 x 26 cm), turquoise C595 (11 x 11 cm) and lily-white C110 (10 x 10 cm) • Pattern 12 • 2 cm wide strips from 4 different blue envelopes from, for example, a government ministry and a school • 3 x 5 cm envelope paper (colour C) • oval (colour A) • Silver deco tape • Hole punch • Small heart hand punch • Foot punch • 30 cm blue ribbon
Punch out the feet. Punch two holes in the front of the dark card for the loop.

Card 5

Card: grey C431 (13 x 26 cm), butter yellow C400 (11 x 11 cm) and lemon yellow C101 (10.3 x 10.3 cm) •

Pattern 12 • 2 cm wide strips from 4 different yellow, grey and white envelopes from, for example, the World Wildlife Fund and a university • 3 x 5 cm envelope (colour C) • oval (colour A) • Rainbow holographic paper • Hole punch • Small heart hand punch • Multi-corner punch • 30 cm light orange ribbon
Punch out two corners of the smallest card.

pattern 12

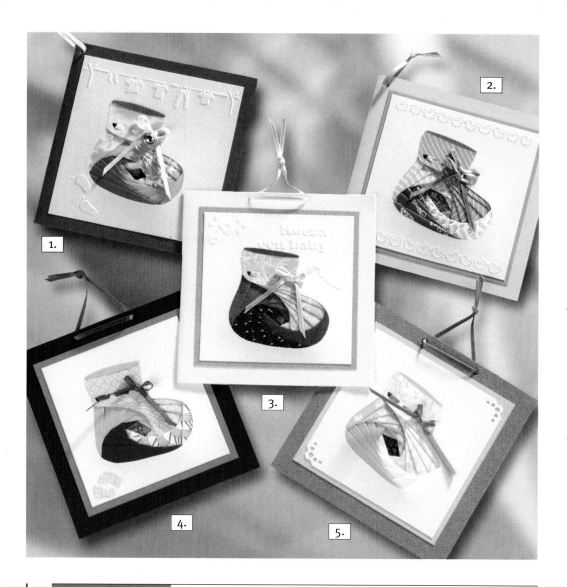

Hearts

Sweethearts

Card 1

Card: light pink C103 (14.8 x 21 cm), cerise P33 (14 x 9.7 cm) and lavender blue C150 (13.8 x 9.4 cm) • Pattern13 • 2 cm strips from 3 blue, grey and red envelopes • Silver deco tape • Heart corner punch
Punch out the corners of the blue card and cut out the heart. IRIS fold the card with the strips.

Card 2

Card: pink A481 (14.8 x 21 cm) • pink C352 (11 x 9.7 cm) and light pink C103 (10 x 9 cm) • Pattern 13 • 2 cm wide strips from 3 different lilac and purple envelopes from, for example, a housing corporation • Silver deco tape • Multi-corner punch
Punch out two corners from the smallest card and cut out the heart at an angle.

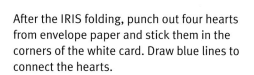

Card 3

Card: violet C502 (14.8 x 21 cm) and shell white C112 (13.7 x 9.4 cm) • Pattern 13 • 2 cm wide strips from 3 different blue and purple envelopes from, for example, a hospital • Silver holographic paper • Multi-corner punch • Blue gel pen

After the IRIS folding, punch out four hearts from envelope paper and stick them in the corners of the white card. Draw blue lines to connect the hearts.

Card 4

Card: pink C352 (14.8 x 21 cm), grey C131 (13.5 x 9.9 cm) and light pink C103 (11.5 x 9.5 cm) • Pattern 13 • 2 cm wide strips from 3 different lilac and pink envelopes • Copper red deco tape • Heart corner punch
Punch out two corners from the smallest card.

Card 5

Card: red C505 (14.8 x 21 cm) and white A211 (12.8 x 9.5 cm) • Pattern 13 • 2 cm wide strips from 3 different orange, red and purple envelopes • Gold holographic paper • Regal corner punch • Ornamental embossing stencil

Cut the corners and cut the heart from the white card. Emboss the red card in the cut-off corners.

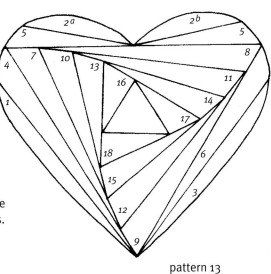

pattern 13

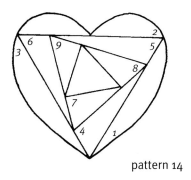

pattern 14

Card 6

Card: shell white C112 (14.8 x 21 cm) and red C505 (13.7 x 9.4 cm) • 2 cm wide strips from 3 different white, yellow and orange envelopes • Gold holographic paper • Small heart hand punch

Cut the heart out of the red card and punch out the small hearts.

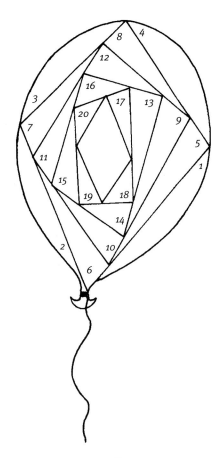

pattern 11

With thanks to:

Kars & Co BV, Ochten, the Netherlands

Koninklijke Talens, Apeldoorn,
the Netherlands
(card material)

CreaArt, Apeldoorn, the Netherlands
For providing the material.

Nederlandse Vereniging voor Papierknip-
kunst (Dutch Society for Paper Cutting Art)
for the cutting tips
Secr. Paulus Potterstraat 3
2162 BS Lisse
The Netherlands

The materials can be ordered by shopkeepers from:

AVEC B.V., Waalwijk, the Netherlands
Kars & Co B.V. Ochten, the Netherlands